MARY ENGELBREIT'S
HOME
COMPANION

Techniques & Ideas

paint

Art & Inspiration

MARY ENGELBREIT'S

HOME COMPANION

Techniques & Ideas

paint

Art & Inspiration

Text by Vitta Poplar

Photography by Barbara Elliott Martin

Andrews McMeel
Publishing

Kansas City

www.andrewsmcmeel.com
www.maryengelbreit.com

Library of Congress Cataloging-in-Publication Data

Engelbreit, Mary
    Paint: techniques & ideas, art & inspiration /text by Vitta Poplar; photography by Barbara Elliott Martin.
       p. cm.
    "Mary Engelbreit's home companion."
    ISBN 0-7407-0029-4 (hardcover)
    1. House painting. 2. Furniture painting. 3. Interior decoration.
  I. Martin, Barbara Elliott. II Mary Engelbreit's home companion. III. Title.
  TT323.P67   1999
  745.7--cc21
                                       99-41051
                                          CIP

MARY ENGELBREIT'S HOME COMPANION
EDITOR IN CHIEF: Mary Engelbreit
EXECUTIVE EDITOR: Barbara Elliott Martin
ART DIRECTOR: Marcella Spanogle

First Edition
10 9 8 7 6 5 4 3 2

PRODUCED BY SMALLWOOD & STEWART, INC., NEW YORK CITY
EDITOR: Carrie Chase
ART DIRECTOR: Debbie Sfetsios

PRINTED IN GREAT BRITAIN BY BUTLER & TANNER LTD., FROME AND LONDON

contents

introduction

I f stepping into a paint store feels a bit like walking into a spinning kaleidoscope, colors everywhere and out of control, your worries are over. There's no reason to be intimidated by paint. It's so much fun to play with, and in this book we'll show you how.

Indeed, one of the wonderful things about paint is that it lets you experiment and make mistakes, and it never tells a soul. You can alter any color to your liking—a few drops of magenta here, burnt umber there, white to lighten up, black to add depth—and try your hand at any technique, most of which are very forgiving. It's that simple. I suspect that one reason so many of us hesitate to pick up a paintbrush is that it seems like there are so many rules about paint.

But it ain't necessarily so. If you need proof, just turn to our Chapter Two profile of Tracy Porter, who uses paint anywhere and in any way she likes. Tracy is one of several wonderful artists we feature within. What they all have in common is a spirit of adventure. I'm sure that when you've seen their work, you'll be tempted to retire your roller (at least for a while) and turn to rags, stamps, sponges, windshield scrapers, even feather dusters, to get the creative one-of-a-kind results that can turn a home from ordinary to spectacular. Happy painting!

Mary Engelbreit

chapter

inspirations
finding your true colors

Mysteries of the spectrum: Cool colors, with their blue/green undertones, keep their distance, ABOVE. Adding hues in the red/yellow family warms a room, OPPOSITE; these "huggers" of the color world come toward you.

here is it written that you must use a paint store's selection of colors? It's important to paint your own picture. But even though there are about a trillion colors to choose from, it still can be hard to find "that one" you dream of. Never mind—you can tint, lighten, deepen, and recombine paint to achieve something entirely new. Of course, deciding on the color you want might be harder than finding or creating it.

Inspiration is everywhere, in stormy skies and ginkgo leaves and an old ballet tutu. Listen to how color speaks to you. If you hear the siren call of the most outrageous shade of purple, answer it. Maybe you'll only use it as an accent in a hallway, but it will make a world of difference.

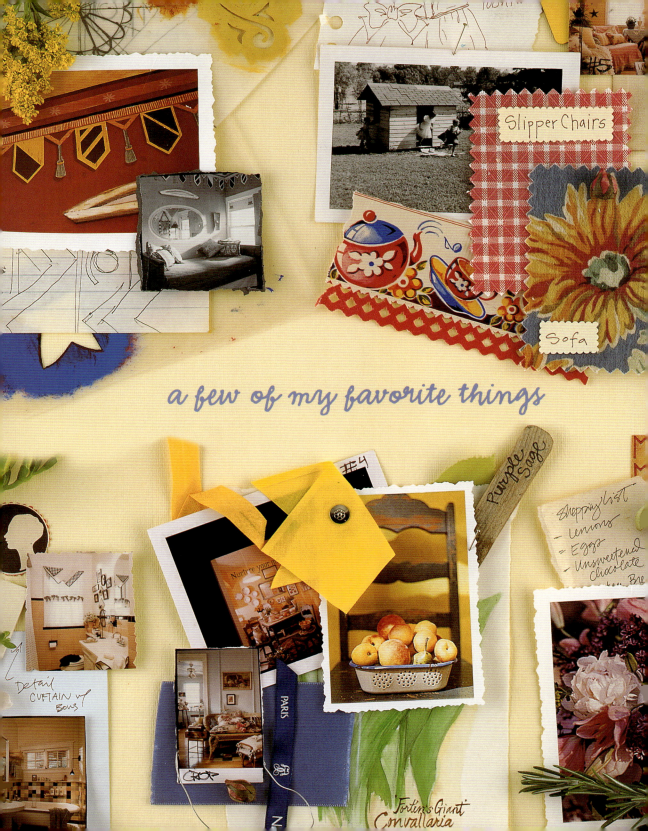

a few of my favorite things

Slipper Chairs

Sofa

#4

Purple Sage

Shopping List
- Lemons
- Eggs
- Unsweetened Chocolate

Nurture your...

Detail
CURTAIN w/
Bows

PARIS

CROP

Fortin's Giant
Convallaria

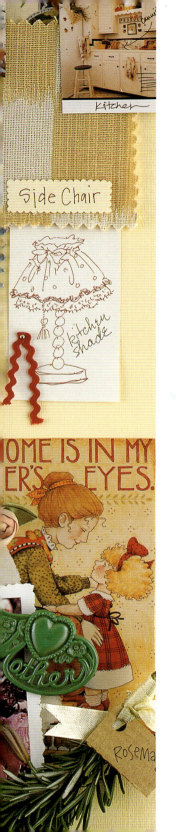

Pin your swatches up on a bulletin board, LEFT, to discover how colors interact. Live with it awhile. Then see how the combinations translate to paint. Or find your inspiration in childhood memories, choosing your favorites from the crayon box, RIGHT.

live in a rainbow

Calling all swatches, keepsakes, and treasures picked up at the beach and on hikes: Swirl them together on a table and see what ends up side by side. Examine them for novel color and texture combinations. Finger a small stone and study its lines and color. Maybe you could replicate the texture in your kitchen, or use the color on a wall in your bath? And that striped fabric would make a wonderful starting point for a painted dining room wall.

Once you start thinking about what color can do in your home, you'll find yourself haunting paint store aisles, tearing pages from magazines, and cutting swatches from fabric. Keep a note-book, colored pencils, and glue stick at the ready to record your discoveries. You'll discover that for a mere pittance (compared to the cost of home furnishings), paint—and color—will completely transform your world.

paint chips will

take you only so far...

Nature doesn't need a color wheel to get it right. Yellow and purple are natural complements—notice how one appears just as an accent, LEFT, further brightening the visual impact of the iris.

With its striking summer sunset shades, ombré ribbon, ABOVE, could easily inspire a colorwashed bedroom wall.

If paint chips seem too intangible, try spools of thread, OPPOSITE. Stack up imaginary rooms, with base-board, wall, and ceiling colors in that order.

Like scoops of pistachio and butter-pecan on the same cone, green and buttery yellow partner each other quite deliciously. The technical explanation is that they're analogous colors.

color marriages made in heaven

Y ou learned it in kindergarten. Start with red, yellow, and blue. Mix them to get orange, violet, or green. Then mix the first batch (red, yellow, and blue) with the second batch (orange, violet, and green). Now it gets really interesting—all those shades like blue-green and yellow-orange. Add some white to lighten them up, a few drops of black to deepen them. Arrange them in a circle and you have the color wheel, which shows how the colors of the spectrum relate to one another.

Work together they do. Merry Christmas—red and green. Don't the daylilies look more vivid next to the larkspur?—orange and blue. These are complementary colors which sit opposite each other on the color wheel and seem to vibrate energetically when used together. Analogous colors, like red and orange, sit next to one another on the color wheel and when paired create visual harmony.

Just when you thought it was safe to turn the page, here's a new term: triadic colors, combinations of three colors that sit equidistant on the color wheel. Blue, red, and yellow are one such trio; in a living room, FAR LEFT, violet—next to blue on the color wheel—throws in a playful twist.

Analogous colors always go together, ABOVE and LEFT.

Blue always has a calming effect, but by contrasting two shades—delft above the chair rail and a paler Wedgwood shade below—an Atlanta homeowner gave her dining room subtle vibrancy. Creamy trim keeps the effect from seeming too cold.

green is

nature's neutral

You can rarely go wrong using a single color, and green is perhaps the easiest of all to use. All its flavors—lime, celery, apple—mix and match. No matter what its intensity, green is such a serene color, it's thought to bring on a contemplative mood. Green also works well no matter what the season— it's natural and fresh in the summer, warm and festive in the winter.

If you need more proof of complementary color synergy, check out this living room. Orange, yellow, blue, and violet all take a turn on different surfaces, and boy do they pop.

If your home is by the ocean—
or even if it isn't—try a
sailboat "canvas" white on
the walls, LEFT, and even the
floor. Furnishings will seem
to float within the space.

   With ivory—indeed, any
shade of white—as a back-
drop, small doses of color
go a long way, RIGHT.

the power of
white

Once you scratch the surface, you'll find that painting things white is not as simple as it seems. White can be as fresh as a Nantucket cottage, or as sleek and elegant as a Parisian townhouse. Pure white is cool. With yellow or beige undertones it becomes warm. That's why color analysts recommend using warm whites in northern-lit rooms and frosty whites in rooms with southern exposures.

   As for eastern- and western-oriented rooms, why not mix it up? In fact, some people layer several whites, using the deepest hue below the chair rail or on the wainscoting, a slightly lighter tint on the upper walls, and the lightest of all on the ceiling, which makes it seem higher. Whatever shade you choose, the effect is always tranquil.

a classic approach

White makes any room seem larger, especially when you mix several shades in vignettes, playing tricks with depth and perspective, ABOVE. When you vary white's finish, the results are as complex as colored patterns. For instance, smooth glossy paint on the walls contrasts with a crackled bed frame and mirror, RIGHT. Paint also plays against textiles—here, the plump chenille pillows.

chapter 2

transforming touc

paint can perk up anything

Paint often picks up where architectural accents and furnishings leave off. In this bedroom, a stencil not only anchors a plate rail and defines a dado, OPPOSITE, but also echoes the lively flounces of bed fabric.

It's all well and good to know the basic principles of the color wheel, but sometimes, you just have to put your own spin on it. If you like the unorthodox but perfectly acceptable combinations of aqua and copper or silver and citrus green, then give them a whirl on your walls. Or furniture. Or stripe them on your floors. Because paint combinations can go just about anywhere.

Use a color where it's least expected. For instance, we all think of pink for a girl's bedroom. But look at a small sampling of its many hues, ABOVE, and study its many moods. Use a bold porcelain pink in your living room, accented by beige woodwork. Paint the inside of your medicine cabinet peony. It will make you happier instantly.

Bold spots of color and a trompe l'oeil countertop base bring spark to a kitchen, LEFT.

Artist Jesse Hickman made and painted a colorful mirror frame, bird sculpture, and doll-house, RIGHT. You could do the same with unfinished wood objects from a craft store.

shout it out
in color

Turn your home into a three-dimensional work of art by painting details everywhere. The kitchen is as good a place to start as any. By sanding the cabinets to give them a good "tooth" and then applying primer, you can paint right over them in any color of the rainbow—no need to be tied to neutrals. Or if your cabinets are glass, paint the inside back wall a vibrant color, like cinnabar or lime.

Add surprise touches of color to alcoves, perhaps one that is home to a bookshelf. A harlequin pattern would be a nice back-drop here, perhaps in purple, crimson, and canary.

Don't forget the floor—add checkerboards, stencils, a border, trailing vines, or a strawberry patch, but remember to preserve what you've done by sealing the results with a few coats of varnish or polyurethane.

When choosing colors for outdoors, think tropical: Bright colors stand up to sunshine best and mix well with foliage and flowers. Use acrylics and sealer or exterior latex for the best resistance to the weather.

Color can go anywhere and do anything

Freehand lettering on a potting shed wall sets an informal mood, LEFT. Lettering can be as easy as painting an old piece of wood (sand away some paint for a distressed feel) and making your statement on top, RIGHT. For a more finished look, use stencils.

a penny for your thoughts

We all clip quotes out of magazines and stick them up on our refrigerators. But if you want more permanent inspiration, paint your message right on the wall.

Artist Marcy Spanogle suggests you look through typography or lettering books to find a typeface you like. Draw a giant version of elementary school lined paper on the wall with a soft pencil, and use it as a guide for the letters. Sketch in an outline of the letters with the pencil—you might want to trace them from an enlarged photocopy. Then thin some acrylic paint with a little water, so it's easy to apply with a small, soft sable paintbrush—a number 3 or 4. Provided you are working on gloss or semigloss walls, you can wipe off mistakes with a wetted paper towel.

After the paint dries, erase the pencil lines with a white gummy eraser.

...THE MANY HOURS, WE'VE SIMPLY S...

Quotes can go anywhere: reading nooks, mantels, foyers. To find suitable sayings, scour rummage and library sales for books of quotations and proverbs. Or letter a child's name over a bed or on a chairback—everyone will know exactly who goes where.

The ornament of a house is the friends who frequent it

Emerson

Intricate as an embroidered Guatemalan blouse, folkloric motifs embellish these dining room chairbacks. For a short-cut, you can use decorative stamping paints and foam blocks to create special details like these.

don't just
sit there

Transforming orphaned chairs into a dining room or kitchen set is one of the most satisfying paint projects. Not only do you get to express yourself artistically, but you're left with very functional, practical results without spending loads of money.

We've all had the experience of spotting old chairs sitting along the side of the road or being sold for next-to-nothing at a flea market. Go for the ones that are basically intact. Sponge clean them with mild soap and water, sand away stains, fill cracks with putty, and cover with primer. Now comes the fun part—bringing them to new, colorful life. Use latex paint for a base coat and the saturated hues of artists' acrylics for the details, whether painted freehand or with stencils. When you're done, protect your work with matte varnish. You don't have to assemble several chairs and make a set—just lavish creativity on a single chair if you please.

Mary Engelbreit gave a little girl's room, LEFT, a polka-dotted personality, painting them on the lighting fixtures and a dresser.

Aluminum buckets become vases when brushed with acrylic paint, RIGHT. Give your mailbox the same treatment.

let's do the polka

P olka dots are one of the quickest and most fun ways to pull a room together. Paint some with a small brush onto secondhand furniture—for instance, a dresser and a nightstand—and suddenly you have a matched set.

Sure, you could make perfectly round and evenly spaced polka dots using an acetate template. But your dots don't have to be exact. Use a paint pen or a pencil eraser tip to stipple them on. (If you're painting dots on metal watering cans or buckets, ABOVE, don't use enamel paint pens, as they'll eat through an acrylic base coat.) Or paint the back of some bubblewrap, then lay it on a surface. Instant pattern!

Kids' rooms and polka dots naturally go together, but don't be afraid to make any room playful. Run a border of dots around the top of the wall where it meets the ceiling or let them bubble up a bathroom door.

Decorative painter Steve Haskamp, whose work appears on these and the following pages, uses flat latex paints sealed with clear varnish to produce striking results.

"Treat doorways and windows as frames to the scene within or beyond," advises Steve. "A good dose of black in a border always gives other colors more resonance."

bordering on the fantastic

Without woodwork, doorways and windows would seem lackluster. Walls would simply sink into the floor. The backbone of a room—moldings, chair rails, and ceiling medallions—deserve a little more consideration than basic white paint, don't you think? Maybe you should go with gold or silver. Have you considered robin's egg blue?

One intriguing option is combing woodwork to produce subtle stripes. Put down a latex base coat color, let it dry, then mix a translucent glaze (try two parts latex paint, one part water, and one part glaze). With a brush, cover the surface with the paint-glaze. Now take a woodgraining comb and pull it through from top to bottom, either holding it straight or moving it gently from side to side to make a squiggle pattern. You could also use the comb on the diagonal to create a crosshatch pattern resembling plaid.

"Use a squiggle to tie it all together."

To top a window frame, Steve combined salt and pepper stippling with bold color blocks, LEFT. "Simple geometric patterns add the most interest and impact per square inch," he says.

Create a border where there is none, ABOVE, or highlight each area of woodwork—for instance, the panels in a door—with a different paint color and motif, RIGHT.

While Tracy and John Porter's outdoor world might be a tad monochromatic at certain times of the year, LEFT, their home enjoys eternal spring and summer, RIGHT.

Tracy Porter
artist at work

Don't mention the color wheel to Tracy Porter. Or ask her about decorating plans. When the home furnishings designer set about transforming a ramshackle Wisconsin farmhouse, her only "plan" was to drive to the paint store: "I chose about fourteen different latex colors, having no idea where they would go. Then I started painting, watering them down, layering them on." Eight years later, every surface, from floors to woodwork to lampshades, bursts with color.

"People ask, 'Where do I begin?' My answer is, in very small ways. You build. Start with just one wall. Tell yourself it's going to be the prettiest petal pink wall you've ever seen in your life. After that, you'll take another step. Not everyone can be an opera star or a great athlete, but anyone can paint beautifully."

Freehand drawings and quotes painted with acrylics wind their way across kitchen cabinets and moldings. Tracy thought the room needed something more, so she decoupaged stickers, post-cards, and magazine cutouts everywhere. On the counter-tops, she sealed the results with a clear pourable resin called Enviro-Tech.

"*I wanted a place to*
be inspired by."

"By ignoring all the rules about paint, you'll find unique ways to use it," advises Tracy. "I'll put latex paint on a lampshade, or floor stain on furniture, and it works out great. And I never measure lettering before I apply it. I just pick up a paintbrush or a marker and go." Tracy's own thoughts enliven a headboard, LEFT, while an e.e. cummings poem drifts across a file cabinet, ABOVE.

Lacy, airy textile stencils look just right in bedrooms. A doily makes a great ready-made template, but you could do something even more elaborate: Stretch a piece of lace on a wooden frame and secure with a staple gun. Have a friend hold the frame against the wall, while you lightly spraypaint right over the pattern.

stenciling

stenciling started out as an inexpensive alternative to wallpaper. Nowadays, it's hardly a compromise. It's more like a revelation. With little more than paint, a brush, and a template, you can completely change the mood of a room.

If your house lacks architectural detail, give it some soul with stenciled gothic trefoils and quatrefoils running around the windows and doors. Or maybe the house is too austere and needs a country touch: Let painted apples bob above your chair rail and checks pattern the dado area beneath.

You could even live in a jewelbox: Paint walls the colors of emeralds, rubies, and sapphires. Then trace copies of symbols from a book of Victorian or medieval decoration and transfer them to cardboard or acetate. Using gold paint, strew them across the walls and ceiling.

Almost any surface takes to stenciling, even a heavy film panel, LEFT, transformed into a screen. The rosettes and swirls were made with acrylic paints.

A diamond stencil with an intricate fleur de lis "anchors" a shelf, ABOVE. More than one technique was used here: The stencil was applied to a ragged wall, and the small gold diamonds were hand-painted on afterward. A mix of interior latex paint, glazing liquid, and universal tints, RIGHT, created the subtle antiqued colors of artist Tom Proch's design.

Mar Gee Farr of Hinsdale, Illinois, turned her plain wood potting shed floor into an oversized bandana in a single day. It's not as difficult as it looks. Here's how it's done: Color the floor with an oil-based porch and deck paint, then stencil on motifs using acrylics, taking care each time you reposition the stencil. Finish with a final coat (or two) of varnish.

stenciling

shopping list

- flat, eggshell, or semigloss interior latex paint for base coat (optional) and stenciling colors

- stencil acetate, permanent marker, and X-Acto® knife (if making your own stencil) OR ready-made stencil

- paint tray and roller (if painting a base coat)

- masking tape or stencil adhesive (available at craft stores)

- stencil brush(es)

- cardboard or paper towels (for blotting)

Though a bit of stencil can go almost anywhere, think about your surface before you begin a stenciling project. Walls or columns are ideal; carved surfaces and moldings are not. If you practice a stencil on paper first and play with the color combinations, you'll feel more confident when you start work.

Virtually every type of paint can be used for stenciling. In general, choose water-based paints (acrylic and latex) for surfaces that won't receive a lot of wear and tear. Use oil-based paints (including japan colors) for frequently touched areas like woodwork.

You can either buy stencils in a craft shop or design and make your own. Books are a great source of stencil design ideas. Look for art books that illustrate historic patterns or clip art books. Textiles are also a great source, and allow you to coordinate stenciled motifs with actual patterns in your home: Lay the fabric on a flat surface, pin or tape it in place, and trace a motif.

how to do it:

make your stencil

Using a pencil, trace your design onto tracing paper. Reduce or enlarge on a copy machine, if necessary. Lay a piece of stencil acetate over the design—leaving a generous border of three inches or so—and hold in place with masking tape. Using a permanent marker, draw the design on the acetate. Cut out the design with an X-Acto® knife. Or use any of the many ready-made stencils available at craft stores.

prepare the surface

With a tray and roller, apply a base coat to the wall. Let dry. If you're not painting, clean with an appropriate cleaner and let dry.

apply the design

Choose a focal point on the wall— a window, a shelf, a mantel—to begin stenciling from. Mark the corners of the stencil around the room lightly with pencil or chalk. With masking tape or stencil adhesive, tape the stencil to the wall at the focal point. With a stencil brush and a contrasting color, begin painting the design. Keep the brush fairly dry: Put a little paint on the ends of the bristles, blot any excess on a piece of cardboard or paper towel, and add color to the cutout areas, using stippling or "pouncing" strokes.

Carefully lift the stencil and, working outward from the focal point, reposition the stencil, using the pencil marks as a guide. Paint the design. Repeat until you've worked your way around the room.

embellish the look

For additional colors, let the area dry before using a new stencil and clean brush.

When you contrast two neutral shades that would otherwise go unnoticed, they suddenly have presence and resonate with one another. Stripes in very similar colors like pale yellow, LEFT, and cream, RIGHT, give a muted, soft effect that works beautifully in a room.

striping

Want to open up a room and lend it height? Striping creates the illusion in a few simple steps. Some people shy away from stripes, thinking that they will create a barred effect. But if you keep the colors analogous, the effect will be stylish and "finished" looking. For instance, alternate light green, dark green, and copper—all colors that have earthy associations—for a look that's tied together, crisp, yet harmonious.

Stripes have a way of evoking summertime, too, with its tumult of beach towels, awnings, and seersucker shirts. An aquatic palette of soft blue and sea green does the trick nicely. Or play with sherbet colors like raspberry and peach—pretty in girl's room. If these stripes are done in a translucent glaze, they will shimmer like a rainbow.

earn your stripes!

Even in the depths of winter, this home retains its light-hearted soul with a playful palette. When making stripes from colors that are closely related like this, contrast flat and satin finishes to add another dimension.

striping

- flat, eggshell, or semigloss interior latex paint for base coat plus 1 or more additional color(s) for striping
- water-based glazing liquid (optional), plastic container, and stirring stick
- paint trays
- 2 rollers for base coat and stripe (no wider than stripe width) OR 1 roller and 1 wide (about 4-inch) brush
- measuring tape
- plumb line and chalk
- straightedge
- low tack painter's tape
- artist's brush (optional)
- rags or sea sponge (optional)

Striping is all about measuring and prep work. When you get to the part where you're actually creating the stripes, most all of the work is already done.

You can approach striping any number of ways. You could apply the stripes with paint straight from the can using a roller. You could apply the paint entirely with a sea sponge or rags for a more textured effect. Or you could use a glazing liquid, with a sponge, rag, or roller, for a subtler effect. Whichever method you choose, read through these instructions fully before starting.

The larger the room, the more stripes it can handle. Stripes that are 4 to 6 inches wide work well for most spaces. Or use one roller width as a measure. Varying stripes of 6, 12, and 18 inches width will produce an interesting color-blocking effect.

As with all projects, it's a good idea to experiment with techniques and formulas on posterboard before you begin.

how to do it:

1 prepare the surface

Clean the wall with an appropriate cleaner. With a tray and roller, apply a base coat to the wall. Let dry.

2 make your marks

Measure the width of the wall and decide on your stripe width. With a ruler and pencil, mark along the top of the wall where the stripes should go. With one person standing on a ladder, drop a plumb line down at the first mark and mark the stripes in increments. With a straightedge and chalk, connect the marks from the ceiling to the floor. Repeat for each stripe. Run painter's tape along the outside edge of each chalk line. Wipe away the chalk.

3 paint the stripes

Either use paint from a can or make a paint-glaze by mixing paint and glazing liquid in a plastic container. Experiment with the formula: You might prefer half glaze, half paint, or you might like a more translucent effect of one part paint to four parts glaze. Pour the paint or paint-glaze into a tray and roll or brush it on between the painter's tape.

4 clean the lines

When the paint or paint-glaze has set but is not completely dry, remove the tape, in quick motions, like you're pulling off a bandage. If any paint has strayed outside the lines, do touch-ups in the base paint color with an artist's brush.

5 a variation

For a very soft stripe, apply the paint or paint-glaze randomly with a brush, then remove with a rag, rubbing most of it away. Or use a sea sponge and apply the paint sparingly.

chapter 3

faux finishes

is it magic? transforming looks

magine taking the most ordinary, light-starved room and turning it into a sun-dappled refuge or an enchanted forest, or giving unfinished off-the-truck furniture an instant history, or imbuing a new home with the look of an ancient Italian villa.

No, you don't have to be a smock-wearing artist living in a garret to perform these miracles (almost) overnight. Some of them—sponging and antiquing in particular—are surprisingly easy, and you can go beyond what we do here: Spatter-paint the walls with a toothbrush, comb a glaze with a window-washing squeegee, or mottle it with a feather duster. So get out your brushes, paints, and, yes, your smock, and prepare to color your world.

Decorative artist Kemit Amenophis created the backdrop for a mural, OPPOSITE, using "an arsenal of sponges" and latex paint mixed with a glaze. He even sponged the tree leaves, then painted in details and highlights with a brush and artist's acrylics. "I keep all brushes, tints, and paints handy, because I never know what I'm going to grab next."

Even in a room with a north-
ern exposure, sponged walls
approximate tricks of natural
daylight, since the color will
naturally vary from wall to wall,
top to bottom. Painted the
color of terra-cotta tile, this
dining room's mottled glow
creates a mellow mood.
Mirrors directly facing one
another on opposite walls
amplify the effects.

sponging

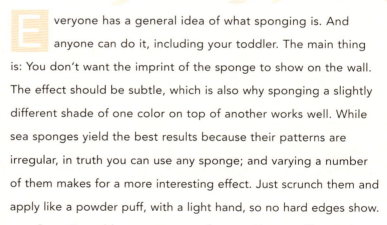

Everyone has a general idea of what sponging is. And
anyone can do it, including your toddler. The main thing
is: You don't want the imprint of the sponge to show on the wall.
The effect should be subtle, which is also why sponging a slightly
different shade of one color on top of another works well. While
sea sponges yield the best results because their patterns are
irregular, in truth you can use any sponge; and varying a number
of them makes for a more interesting effect. Just scrunch them and
apply like a powder puff, with a light hand, so no hard edges show.

Sponging adds texture to a surface, and it sets off artwork
without being too busy. You might not be able find the exact
match of wallpaper to show off crisp black-and-white silhouettes
or a landscape painting, but sponging lets you create the perfectly
mottled background, with as much (or as little) color as you like.

Pick out a color or two from your furnishings, as Mary did in her home office, LEFT, and then apply it to the wall as a sponged motif—it's an instant way to pull a room together. Another unsung advantage of sponging is that it effectively camouflages wall defects. For instance, plaster walls, ABOVE, are naturally uneven, but with a sponged finish they take on the look of a Roman villa.

take the sponge plunge

Prized pieces of a plate
collection displayed on a
dresser, ABOVE, and over
a window, RIGHT, seem
even pinker in a bedroom
sponged to resemble cotton
candy. Sponging is a neutral
backdrop, so it combines
easily with other painted
motifs, like the freehand
flowers in this room.

sponging

shopping list

- flat interior latex paint for base coat
- 1 or more color(s) flat, eggshell, or semigloss interior latex paint for sponging
- water-based glazing liquid
- roller, paint trays (1 for each color), and stirring sticks
- a variety of sea and/or household sponges
- plastic containers
- newspaper or paper towels for blotting

With sponging, less is always more—at first. You just want to dip the sponge lightly into the paint-glaze, then dab off any excess on paper towels. Work from top to bottom and gather enough sponges so that you have one for every color you use. Remember, the lighter your palette, the more forgiving your results (a handy rule that applies to all painting projects). Keep in mind too that when sponging in several colors, the one on top (last used) tends to predominate; as a rule, most professionals work from dark to light. This doesn't apply to the base coat, however, which is generally lighter—perhaps the same color as the final sponging coat.

The only tricky thing is getting into those corners: Cut up a sponge just for this purpose.

As with all projects, it's a good idea to experiment with techniques and formulas on posterboard before you begin.

how to do it:

1  prepare the surface

Clean the wall with an appropriate cleaner. With a tray and roller, apply a base coat to the wall. Let dry.

2  mix the paint

In a container, make a paint-glaze by mixing a sponging paint with glazing liquid. Experiment with the formula: You might prefer half glaze, half paint, or you may want to go for a more translucent effect of one part paint to four parts glaze. Pour the paint-glaze into a tray.

3  apply the paint

Moisten and wring out a sponge. Dip the sponge into the paint-glaze, then dab off excess on newspaper or paper towels. Begin in an unobtrusive area of the wall, starting at the top and working to the bottom in vertical bands. Apply in a quick dabbing motion, being careful not to smudge. Don't overwork areas—keep moving. Turn the sponge around in your hand regularly, apply varying pressure on it, and change directions for different effects. Avoid filling in all areas exactly the same.

4  add layers

When you've sponged on your first layer and it is dry (most likely by the time you've finished a wall), you may want to sponge a new color of paint-glaze over it. The goal is not to completely cover what you've done: Remember to let the bottom color(s) show through.

5  evaluate the look

Step back and survey your work. Some areas will be lighter than others, but in general there should be a balanced look that doesn't fade markedly from dark to light, unless you're setting up a background for a mural and you want the "land" to be darker than the "sky." You can repair a sponged area by going back over it with one of the light colors that you've used.

Its carved and molded areas selectively sanded down, this mirrored buffet, LEFT, looks like a much-loved family heirloom.

Scratches on this table's sides and base could have been put there a century ago, or yesterday, RIGHT.

antiquing

Have you ever been tempted by a table you've found at a yard sale? It might not be terribly old, but it has these wonderful curved legs with graceful neoclassical lines. A different finish would truly make it look like an antique. And that cabinet you picked up at the unfinished furniture store also has potential: With a little distressing and some chicken wire to replace the door panels, you could have yourself an old-fashioned pie safe.

Antiquing is a way of making something new look like it's been around forever, transforming something plain into a piece with character, or letting something truly old show off its history. The key is to tell yourself a story about the piece. Where has it been? How was it handled? Imagine where the wear and tear would be—like on a wooden chair's arms—and let the paint finish flow from there.

You can simulate an aged look on mirror frames with silverleaf, OPPOSITE—apply a base coat of black spray-paint, add gold sizing, which is a sticky varnish, and then apply silver leaf. When dry, brush off the loose bits.

Sanding away at old wood-work reveals generations of paint underneath, ABOVE and RIGHT. Called pentimento, this process creates an instant farmhouse look.

antiquing

shopping list

BOTH PROJECTS:

- paint stripper (liquid or paste)
- gloves, safety mask, and goggles
- putty knife
- sandpaper
- sandpaper block (optional)
- paintbrush
- sponges for cleaning

PENTIMENTO:

- varnish (McCloskey's Heirloom Varnish is ideal)

YARD-SALE FIND:

- water-based primer
- 2 or more colors flat, eggshell, or semigloss interior latex paint for base coat and layer(s)
- 2-inch paintbrush

Transforming a piece of furniture into an "antique" takes a bit of elbow grease, but you'll love the results. There are essentially two methods of antiquing—taking off layers or adding on layers. Both of them call for paint stripper, which is quite toxic—so work in a well-ventilated area and take heed of the manufacturer's warnings.

When a piece of furniture is really thick with old paint—typical of old cabinets—become an archaeologist by going on a dig into the pentimento—the layers. Then seal the exposed layers of paint, marbled in swirls and patches of color, under several coats of varnish for a lacquered effect.

For furniture that isn't covered with layers and layers of paint—perhaps a yard-sale discovery—create the layers yourself and then add an antique finish.

how to do it:

uncovering pentimento

Remove drawers, hinges, and knobs from furniture pieces, or cover with masking tape. In a well-ventilated area, use paint stripper to remove some of the paint. Leave the paint stripper on long enough that the paint loosens, but not so long that it removes the paint entirely.

With a putty knife, scrape away whatever paint comes loose. Sand all over the piece, exposing the layers of pre-existing paint. With a damp sponge, wipe the surface with mild soap and water. Let dry.

With a paintbrush, apply a coat of varnish. Let dry.

Sand again lightly to get rid of bubbles and dust, creating a satin finish. Wipe the surface with a damp sponge, let dry, and apply another layer of varnish. Repeat this process as many as three times.

transforming a yard-sale find

Remove drawers, hinges, and knobs from furniture pieces, or cover with masking tape. In a well-ventilated area, use paint stripper to remove all the paint. Follow the directions and be patient—let the stripper do the work. Use a putty knife to remove the paint, and then sand away whatever still sticks. Wipe with a damp sponge. Let dry.

With a paintbrush, apply a coat of primer. Let dry.

With a 2-inch paintbrush, apply a base coat of paint. Let dry. Apply another color of paint over the base. Let dry. Repeat with a third color, if you like, and let dry.

Use a fine grade of sandpaper to sand areas of the piece that would typically receive wear, exposing some of the base paint as well as the original wood.

Inspired by a Roman fresco in the Metropolitan Museum of Art in New York, artist Tom Proch set out to recreate the look in his bedroom. With washcloth in hand, Tom slathered on a transparent wash of latex paint mixed with glazing liquid and water. "For the entire room, I used about a three-quarters cup of paint," he reveals.

ragging

Most people use artwork and furnishings to keep the eye moving around a room, but paint can do the same thing, especially when you use a ragging technique on the walls. Ragging gives walls a soft, fluid look, a sense of movement. And it looks like it's been there forever.

For Texas-based decorative painter Tom Proch, ragging is the answer when he wants to create a vintage mood. "Don't worry too much about getting the exact right color out of the can," he says. "You're going to be adding glaze, tinting it, or even watering it down, so the color is going to change. Whenever I come across an interesting paint color in the store, I grab it—even if I don't know how I'm going to use it. I just know it'll come in handy the moment inspiration strikes."

Welcome to "the pink room," Tom's Tuscan fantasy. "It all began when I found a can of this funny coppery paint in the garage. When I watered it down, I came to this clear base of pink—a single color looks so different when you break down the pigments." Tom ragged the pink on the walls, followed by white, then a touch of brown, all of it smudged with a damp cloth.

ragging

- flat interior latex paint for base coat
- 1 or more colors flat, eggshell, or semigloss interior latex paint for ragging
- paint trays (1 for each color) and 1 or 2 rollers
- plastic containers
- stirring stick(s)
- water-based glazing liquid
- rags (1 for each ragging color): any soft cotton, such as an old T-shirt, or cheesecloth
- paper towels for blotting

There are two basic ways to rag: a positive process (ragging on) and a negative process (ragging off). Ragging on tends to produce a subtler look. With ragging off, you remove paint from the wall almost as soon as you apply it, so work in sections, or be sure to schedule enough time to get the whole room done in one fell swoop.

Keep track of the paint-glaze formulas you create by starting a paint "recipe" book where you can jot down the combinations. Refer to it later for touch-ups, or if you want to create a similar effect in another room. Like sponging, a ragging effect can be obvious, so it's good to use colors that are close in tone.

As with all projects, it's a good idea to experiment with techniques and formulas on posterboard before you begin.

how to do it:

ragging on

1 Clean the wall with an appropriate cleaner. With a tray and roller, apply a base coat to the wall. Let dry.

2 In a container, make a paint-glaze by mixing paint with glazing liquid. Experiment with the formula: You might prefer half glaze, half paint, or you may want to go for a more translucent effect of one part paint to four parts glaze. Pour the paint-glaze into a tray.

3 Moisten and wring out a rag. Twist the rag into a tube-like shape (kind of like a croissant). Dip the rag into the paint-glaze, blot it on paper towels, and, working from top to bottom, roll the rag directly on the wall, starting near a corner (have smaller pieces of rag on hand for getting into the corners themselves). Maintain a continuous wet edge of paint on the wall so that there are no hard demarcation lines.

Change direction often to avoid patterns.

When the rag runs out of paint-glaze, dip again.

4 After the paint has dried, you can layer another color on top of the first, following the same process.

ragging off

Follow steps 1 and 2 above.

3 Work with a friend: One person applies the paint-glaze to the wall with a roller. The other uses a damp, wrung-out rag to take it off, starting in a corner and working from top to bottom. Keep turning the rag around, rolling it directly on the wall. Reshape often and blot off excess paint on paper towels.

4 Add touches of another color with an additional rag if you like.

To create a starry night in a children's loft, artist Rasa Arbas painted the walls and ceiling off-white, then layered transparent glazes of blue and chartreuse. Next, she drew freehand stencils for the stars on parchment paper, cut them out, outlined their varying shapes on the ceiling, and filled each star in with sheets of 22-karat gold leaf.

glazing

There's a certain mystique surrounding glazes. Think of a glaze as paint before color has been added, though its slightly different composition dries to a harder finish than ordinary paint. This is why you don't need to seal glaze-based projects with polyurethane (though you can in high-traffic areas). A glaze slows a paint's drying time, letting you play with it more, while also extending the paint itself. This magic substance—which can be oil- or water-based—also imparts translucency, so you can see through the sheer painted layers.

While most projects in this book require a glaze, glazing is also a technique unto itself—with endless results. It's a way of freshening up a room with hints of lavender and lime, or of adding warmth with tints of gold and apricot. It also creates the dreamy look of age, with siennas and burnt umbers applied as softly as whispers.

"When you look at a well-done glaze, you're aware not of the individual colors, but of the overall effect," says Rasa. In this California living room, the artist employed four warmly tinted glazes: gold, mahogany, umber, and verdigris.

"Glazes should only whisper."

glazing

shopping list

- oil- or water-based flat, eggshell, or semigloss interior paint for base coat
- 3 to 6 additional paint colors (oil- or water-based—to match the base coat) OR universal tints (for both oil- and water-based paints) OR artist's oils from a tube (for oil-based paint only)
- glazing liquid (oil- or water-based—to match the base coat)
- turpentine or other paint thinner (if using oil-based paint)
- paint tray and roller
- plastic container and stirring sticks
- paintbrushes and/or rags for applying glaze
- metallic or iridescent powders (optional; available at art supply stores)

Think of preparing a glaze the way you make a salad—you can add any number of ingredients to get it just right. A glaze can be colored with universal tints (concentrated paints that come in small tubes and can tint all water- and oil-based paint), artists' oils, even metallic powders. Some people feel that oil glazes are more luminous and add depth—giving the impression that you're looking beyond the layers of color. On the other hand, oil takes a long time to dry (it can be days!) and cleanup is messier than with latex paints (you need turpentine, as opposed to water).

See how a posterboard practice sample of glaze combinations looks in the room: "Hold it against different walls at different times of day," recommends Rasa Arbas. "This is when I do my final 'tuneup' board samples—in the room where the finish will cover the walls, so that I can see how color is reflected or diffused by the furnishings."

how to do it:

prepare the surface

Clean the wall with an appropriate cleaner. With a tray and roller, apply a base coat to the wall. Let dry.

mix the glazes

In plastic containers, mix 3 to 6 glazes: Add paint to the glazing liquid until you get the color you're after: The more glaze, the more translucency. The more paint, the more opacity. A general formula is 2 parts paint, 2 parts glaze, and 1 part thinner (water if you're working with latex paint; paint thinner, such as turpentine, if you're working with oil-based paint), but experiment to find the combination you like best. Mix well so you don't get clumps of concentrated color.

If you're using universal tints instead of paint, add a drop of tint at a time into the liquid glaze and stir.

For special effects, add metallic or iridescent powders to the mixture.

apply the glazes

Work with a friend to keep a fluid wash of glaze on the wall with no hard demarcation lines: one person on a ladder and the other person below. Use paintbrushes and apply the glaze in broad, random strokes. Or use rags, dipping the different edges of the rag into a variety of colors at once and wiping them across the wall, like you're polishing it. Then trade off positions: One person might be working with a heavier hand, so this will create a balance.

evaluate the look

Let the walls dry overnight. With a fresh eye, take a look the next day and see which areas, if any, need more glazing.

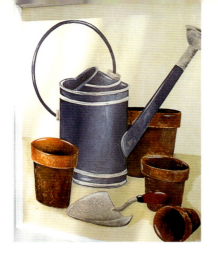

Get all the details down on a drawing pad first, then transfer your still-life to the walls with tracing paper, as a gardener did in her workroom, LEFT.

A sponged yellow background provides the transition from "land" to "sky," RIGHT.

trompe l'oeil

It's time to put it all together: stripes, sponging, ragging, stenciling. You can use all of these techniques in tandem to create beautiful, intricate scenes that fool the eye.

Trompe l'oeil murals are the ultimate decorative painting technique, but their sheer size can be intimidating. Rasa Arbas offers some gentle advice: "Just shrink the size. When I do a mural, I always create a maquette. An eight- by ten-foot wall becomes an eight- by ten-inch drawing. I'll draw and paint the scene, make the colors as accurate as possible, and work out my mistakes here, rather than on the wall. Then I'll project the image large on the wall and trace it with pencil. You have to organize the space so you can deal with it one section at a time."

Rasa also recommends creating murals on large canvas cloths, so they're portable from room to room, house to house.

For realistic skies, experiment with colors other than blue and white: go with pinks, violets, even browns. Rather than starting with a blue, artists Ed Pinson and Debrah Ware added it last, peeking out in patches. While they were at it, they gave the woodwork some golden sunset drama.

Even novice painters can master a faux ribbon, OPPOSITE and ABOVE. Experiment with painting twists and shadows on posterboard first. Lay down the pale base coat of the ribbon and let dry. Then come in with a finer tipped brush using slightly deeper colors to create the shadows.

Your freehand painting skills needn't be flawless to create vines scaling your walls: Instead, pick up a foam stamp kit from a crafts store. Using acrylics and a foam roller, stamp leaves on the wall to create a handpainted effect like Joseph Slattery's handiwork in Mary's front hall, RIGHT.

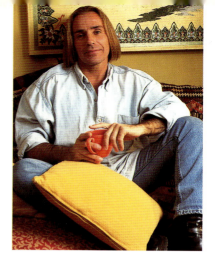

On Francisco's canvas paintings, LEFT, he creates texture by building up layers of acrylics mixed with unusual ingredients like sand and molding paste. The results can resemble fine fabric.

Francisco Casabal Sastre

artist at work

When I came to this country, I was the classic starving artist," remembers Argentine native Francisco Casabal Sastre, now a resident of Dallas. "So I didn't have lots of money to furnish my new apartment. Painting was the solution."

Following the old rule of thumb of starting at the top and working to the bottom, Francisco began with the ceiling, painting mandalas with an Egyptian theme. Astonishingly intricate, they force the question: How did you get them so perfect?

"I traced over designs in a mythology book and adjusted the details to my own liking," he reveals. "Then I blew them up to size, transferred them to acetate, and made my own stencils." Since then, Francisco has been using homemade multipart stencils to paint everything from monkeys to Egyptian kings.

There are no shortcuts to
achieving the rich colors and
ancient look of Francisco's
murals. He uses the tech-
nique of true fresco, in which
pigments are mixed with
damp plaster and become a
part of the wall structure,
rather than sitting on top like
paint. "Then I'll scratch
away at the surface to get
that aged look."

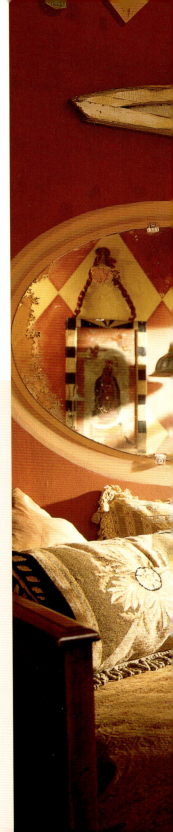

"If you're going to paint ancient motifs or scenes of other cultures, visit museums to see examples of the real thing," Francisco advises. "I do quite a bit of historical research before I pick up a brush. Getting the colors right is probably the most important thing of all."

resources

supplies

Ace Hardware
(630) 990-6600
acehardware.com
Interior and exterior paint

Adele Bishop Design
3430 South Service Road
Burlington, ON L7N 3T9
Canada
(800) 510-0245
Pre-cut stencils and supplies

Benjamin Moore & Co.
51 Chestnut Ridge Road
Montvale, NJ 07645
www.benjaminmoore.com
(800) 826-2623
Interior and exterior paint and stains

Binney & Smith, Inc.
1100 Church Lane
Easton, PA 18044
(800) 272-9652
www.crayola.com
Acrylic paint and artist's brushes

Chatham Art Distributors
(800) 822-4747
Catalog; decorative paints and stains, brushes for furniture

Createx Colors
14 Airport Park Road
East Granby, CT 06026
(800) 243 2712
Catalog; textile paints and dyes

DecoArt
P.O. Box 386
Stanford, KY 40484
(800) 367-3047
Acrylic paint, stencil paint

Delta Technical Coatings, Inc.
2550 Pellissier Place
Whittier, CA 90601-1505
(800) 423-4135
Acrylic paint, stencils and stencil supplies, clear glaze

Dick Blick Art Materials
P.O. Box 1267
Galesburg, IL 61402-1267
(800) 828-4548
www.dickblick.com
Paint supplies

Duron Paints
10406 Tucker Street
Beltsville, MD 20705
(800) 723-8766
Interior and exterior paint

Dutch Boy Paint
101 Prospect Avenue
14 Midland Building
Cleveland, OH 44115
(800) 828-5669
Interior and exterior paint

Finnaren & Haley, Inc.
901 Washington Street
Conshohocken, PA 19428
(800) 843-9800
Interior and exterior paint

Friendly Stencils
590 King Street
Hanover, MA 02339
(781) 878-7596
Stencils

The Furniture Wizard
www.furniturewizard.com
Books, videos, and supplies for furniture repair and refinishing

The Glidden Co.
925 Euclid Avenue
Cleveland, OH 44115
(216) 344-8000
Interior and exterior paint

Helen Foster Stencils
71 Main Street
Sanford, ME 04073
(207) 490-2625
Arts & Crafts–style stencils

HomeRight
www.homeright.com
HomeRight products include pretaped poly drop cloths for masking trim and specialty rollers and brushes

Johnson Paint Co., Inc.
355 Newbury Street
Boston, MA 02115
(800) 404-8114
(617) 536-4838
www.johnson.com
Paint supplies

M.A.B. Paint
(800) 622-1899
Interior and exterior paint

Martin Seynour Paint
101 Prospect Avenue
14 Midland Building
Cleveland, OH 44115
(800) 677-5270
Interior and exterior paint

Paint and Decorating Retailers Association
www.pdra.org
Web site answers FAQs on paint

Pearl Paint Co., Inc.
308 Canal Street
New York, NY 10013-2572
catalog, (800) 221-6845
www.pearlpaint.com
Paint supplies

Plaid Enterprises, Inc.
1649 International Court
PO Box 7600
Norcross, GA 30091-7600
www.plaidonline.com
(800) 842-4197
Acrylic paint, rollers, stencils

Pratt & Lambert Paints
101 Prospect Avenue
14 Midland Building
Cleveland, OH 44115
(800) 289-7728
Interior and exterior paint

Ralph Lauren Paint
101 Prospect Avenue
14 Midland Building
Cleveland, OH 44115
(800) 379-7656
Interior paint, unique finishes, stencil sets

Ritins Studio Series
Toronto, Canada
(416) 467-8920
www.ritins.com
Instruction, field trips to Europe, and mail-order line of decorative paint materials, including glazes and metallic gold, silver, and copper sheets

Sherwin-Williams Co.
101 Prospect Avenue
14 Midland Building
Cleveland, OH 44115
(800) 474-3794
Interior and exterior paint and accessories

Stencil House of N.H.
P.O. Box 16109
Hooksett, NH 03106
(603) 625-1716
Catalog ($4.50, refundable with order); full line of stencil accessories

Texas Art Supply
2001 Montrose
Houston, TX 77006
(713) 526-5221
Paint supplies

Yowler & Shepps Stencils
3529 Main Street
Conestoga, PA 17516
(717) 872-2820
Catalog ($5, refundable with order); stencils for murals and borders, including picket fences, birds, and morning glories

decorative artists

Kemit Amenophis through Floreal
533 Taylor Street
San Francisco, CA 94102
(415) 885-4261
Murals and other special effects

Rasa Arbas Design
306 22nd Street
Santa Monica, CA 90402
(310) 828-3761
Decorative painting, including glazing, murals, and canvases

Francisco Casabal Sastre
4709 Denton Drive
Dallas, TX 75219
(214) 559-3440
www.metronet.com/~casabal
Decorative painting, including murals, art on canvas

Pinson & Ware Painted Ornament
624 E. Foothill Blvd.
Monrovia, CA 93016
(818) 359-6113
Decorative painting

Tracy Porter: The Home Collection
N5373 County W
Princeton, WI 54968
(920) 295-0142
Home accessories inspired by paint techniques

Tom Proch
Fredericksburg, TX 78624
(830) 997-6919
Decorative painting, including antiquing and stenciling, faux finishes; artist-designed stencils by mail order

Joseph Slattery
3825 Botanical Ave. #2
St. Louis, MO 63110
(314) 865-2282
Decorative painting

mary engelbreit stores

Saint Louis
Saint Louis Galleria
1142 St. Louis Galleria
St. Louis, MO 63117
(314) 863-5522

Atlanta
North Point Mall
1212 North Point Circle
Alpharetta, GA 30022
(770) 667-0414

Denver
Cherry Creek Mall #258
3000 East 1st Avenue
Denver, CO 80206
(303) 331-8062

Chicago
Woodfield Shopping Center
N-130 Woodfield Shopping Center
Shaumburg, IL 60173
(847) 240-1444

Dallas
Dallas Galleria
13350 Dallas Parkway, Suite 2820
Dallas, TX 75240
(972) 716-0644

Minneapolis
Mall of America
160 West Market
Bloomington, MN 55425
(612) 854-8860

credits

So many wonderful, creative people have brought us into their homes to inspire you and me. I would like to thank them all from the bottom of my heart.

Mary

PHOTOGRAPHY ON PAGES 18-19 BY BRAD SIMMONS; PAGE 28 BY TRICIA SHAY; PAGES 30, 77, 100-105 BY JENIFER JORDAN; PAGE 34 BY BILL HOLT; PAGES 62-63 BY CHERYL DALTON. ALL OTHER PHOTOGRAPHY BY BARBARA ELLIOTT MARTIN.

2   HOMEOWNERS: Dominique and Patrick Pfahl, San Francisco, California; ARTISAN: Kemit Amenophis, San Francisco, California

8   HOMEOWNER: Bianca Juarez, Los Angeles, California

9   HOMEOWNER, ARTISAN: Jesse Hickman, Petoskey, Michigan

11   HOMEOWNER: Stacey Lamb, Lawrence, Kansas; ARTISAN: Steve Haskamp, Lawrence, Kansas

12   top: ARTISAN: Nancy Wiley, Hudson Valley, New York

bottom: HOMEOWNERS: Susan and Steve Smith, St. Louis, Missouri

13   ARTISAN: Salley Mavor, Cape Cod, Massachusetts

15   HOMEOWNER: Mary Engelbreit, St. Louis, Missouri; ARTISAN: Joseph Slattery, St. Louis, Missouri

16-17   HOMEOWNER: Mary Engelbreit, St. Louis, Missouri

18-19   HOMEOWNER: Pat Collier, Atlanta, Georgia

20-21   HOMEOWNERS: Jane and Steve Keltner, Memphis, Tennessee

22-23   HOMEOWNERS: Julie and Henry Kelston, Nyack, New York

25   HOMEOWNER: Jeff Jones, Atlanta, Georgia

26   HOMEOWNER: Rose Hicks, Fredericksburg, Texas

27   HOMEOWNER: Candy Rosen, Laguna Beach, California

28   ARTISANS: Susan Alexander and Taffnie Bogart, Milwaukee, Wisconsin

29   HOMEOWNERS: Janet and Tom Proch, Fredericksburg, Texas; ARTISAN: Tom Proch

30   HOMEOWNER, ARTISAN: Francisco Casabal Sastre, Dallas, Texas

31   HOMEOWNER, ARTISAN: Jesse Hickman, Petoskey, Michigan

32-33   HOMEOWNERS: Joann and Jim Mattis, Seagrove Beach, Florida. Insets: Birdhouses painted by Mary Engelbreit

34   HOMEOWNERS: Barbara and Rob Kiker, Spokane, Washington

35   HOMEOWNERS: Lacy and Bob Buck, Carmel, California

36   top: HOMEOWNER: Mary Engelbreit, St. Louis, Missouri

bottom: HOMEOWNERS: Janet and Tom Proch, Fredericksburg, Texas

37   HOMEOWNER: Mary Engelbreit, St. Louis, Missouri

38-39   HOMEOWNER: Jennifer Myers, Austin, Texas

index